IF ONE CAN DESTROY EVERYTHING, WHY CAN'T ONE GIRL CHANGE IT?
I AM
NOBEL
PEACE

FIGHT FOR THE THINGS THAT YOU CARE ABOUT.

We Can Do It!
We Can Do It!
WE CAN DO IT!
We Can Do It!
We Can Do It!

We Can Do It!
We Can Do It!
We Can Do It!
We Can Do It!

MARCH
MARCH
DREAMING, AFTER ALL, IS A FORM OF PLANNING.
MARCH
MARCH
MARCH

We Shall overcome
MARCH
MARCH
MARCH
MARCH
MARCH
MARCH
MARCH

WE MAY ENCOUNTER MANY DEFEATS BUT WE MUST NOT BE DEFEATED.

THE FUTURE BELONGS TO THOSE WHO BELIEVE IN THE BEAUTY OF THEIR DREAMS.

USA
USA
USA
USA
USA

FLOTUS
THERE IS
FLOTUS
NO LIMIT
TO WHAT
FLOTUS
WE AS
FLOTUS
WOMEN
CAN
ACCOMPLISH.
FLOTUS
PRESIDENT OF THE USA
PRESIDENT OF THE USA
PRESIDENT OF THE USA

FLOTUS
FLOTUS
FLOTUS
PRESIDENT OF THE USA
FLOTUS
PRESIDENT OF THE USA
FLOTUS
PRESIDENT OF THE USA
FLOTUS
FLOTUS
FLOTUS
PRESIDENT OF THE USA

VOTES FOR WOMEN
LIBERTY 1979
INDEPENDENCE IS HAPPINESS

VOTES FOR WOMEN
LIBERTY 1979

CHANGE YOUR
LIFE TODAY.
DON'T GAMBLE
ON THE
FUTURE,
ACT NOW,
WITHOUT
DELAY.

FIGHT THE
BIG
FIGHTS.
DON'T
FIGHT
THE LITTLE
FIGHT.
NEWS
NEWS
NEWS
NEWS
NEWS

NEWS
NEWS
NEWS
NEWS
NEWS
NEWS
NEWS
NEWS

IF NOT ME, WHO?
IF NOT NOW, WHEN?

TURN
YOUR
WOUNDS
INTO
WISDOM.
OWN

OWN